Words that appear in **bold** type are defined in the glossary on pages 28 and 29.

Please visit our web site at: www.garethstevens.com
For a free color catalog describing Gareth Stevens Publishing's
list of high-quality books and multimedia programs, call
1-800-542-2595 (USA) or 1-800-387-3178 (Canada).
Gareth Stevens Publishing's fax: (414) 332-3567.

Library of Congress Cataloging-in-Publication Data

Baumbusch, Brigitte.
    Eyes in art / by Brigitte Baumbusch.
        p. cm. — (What makes a masterpiece?)
    Includes index.
    ISBN 0-8368-4445-9 (lib. bdg.)
    1. Eyes in art—Juvenile literature. I. Title.
    N8217.E9B38   2005
    704.9'4961184—dc22   2004056703

This edition first published in 2005 by
Gareth Stevens Publishing
A WRC Media Company
330 West Olive Street, Suite 100
Milwaukee, Wisconsin 53212 USA

Copyright © Andrea Dué s.r.l. 2000

This U.S. edition copyright © 2005 by Gareth Stevens, Inc.
Additional end matter copyright © 2005 by Gareth Stevens, Inc.

Translator: Erika Pauli

Gareth Stevens series editor: Dorothy L. Gibbs
Gareth Stevens art direction: Tammy West

Printed in the United States of America

1 2 3 4 5 6 7 8 9 09 08 07 06 05

EYES
in Art

by Brigitte Baumbusch

GARETH**STEVENS**
GS
PUBLISHING
A WRC Media Company

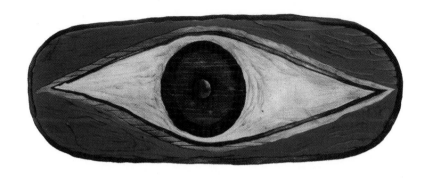

What makes an eye . . .

The eye above is from a painted wooden mask that is about one hundred years old. It was made by the Nootka Indians from Vancouver Island, in Canada.

The small **idol** below has a head that is all eyes. It is almost six thousand years old. This idol, and many others like it, were found at an **ancient** temple in the **Middle East**.

These eyes seem to have a life of their own.
They are part of a large picture painted in
1941 by Spanish artist Joan Miró.

a masterpiece?

Eyes usually come in pairs, but they are . . .

Swiss artist Paul Klee painted this round head with crooked red eyes in 1922.

Wooden masks, like this one (left), were made by the **Inuit** people of Alaska more than one hundred years ago.

Drawings by Jerzy Panek, a contemporary Polish artist, feature four heads, all with different eyes.

not always alike . . .

and sometimes, there are . . .

The wooden mask above has three pairs of eyes. It was made by the Kwele people, who live in the Democratic Republic of the Congo, in Africa.

The little head with four eyes (left) is a **bronze figurine** made in Sardinia more than 2,700 years ago. It represents a **mythical** warrior who was **endowed** with **divine** gifts.

Eight eyes surround a face with two eyes in a magical book from nineteenth-century Ethiopia. This painting might have been intended to **depict** a **cherub**.

more than two!

Eyes can be round . . .

The large green head of this little **jade** figure (left) is tilted to one side and has two **mother-of-pearl** circles for eyes. It is a **pendant** that the Maori people of New Zealand wore around their necks as an **amulet**.

square . . .

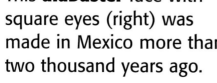

This **alabaster** face with square eyes (right) was made in Mexico more than two thousand years ago.

diamond-shaped . . .

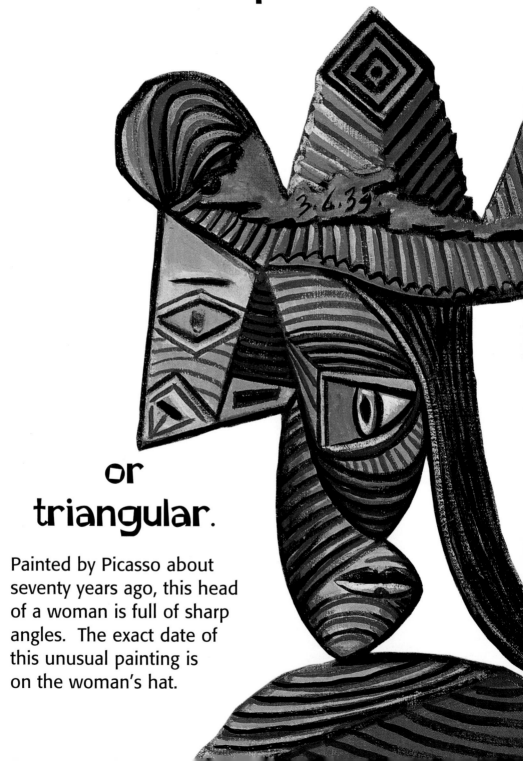

or
triangular.

Painted by Picasso about
seventy years ago, this head
of a woman is full of sharp
angles. The exact date of
this unusual painting is
on the woman's hat.

Some eyes are dreamy . . .

Dante Gabriel Rossetti was an English artist of Italian **origins** who lived in the nineteenth century. Rossetti wrote poetry, and he also painted this **portrait** of a blue-eyed woman lost in thought.

With its eyes opened wide, a tiger watches for **prey** in this Japanese painting from the mid-nineteenth century.

and some are wary.

Some eyes are sunny . . .

Sometimes, the rising Sun looks like a gigantic eye of light – the great eye of the sky. Norwegian artist Edvard Munch painted it that way in the early 1900s.

In the **Middle Ages**, church windows made of colored glass often had figures that could be seen when the Sun shone through. This face of Christ, which is almost a thousand years old, was part of a **stained glass** church window.

some dark.

Sometimes, eyes are precious . . .

An eye made of costly precious gems surrounds the face of a watch designed fifty years ago by Salvador Dalí. Although best known, perhaps, as a **contemporary** Spanish painter, Dalí did art of all kinds.

The golden eyes on this helmet were probably meant to frighten the enemy. The helmet was made in Romania almost 2,400 years ago.

The eyes of this **ivory** goddess are precious rubies. The **statuette** is from Mesopotamia (now Iraq). It was made in about the same time period as the golden helmet above.

and
sometimes . . .

The eyes peering out from behind
the **watercolor** below are carved
on the end of a wooden club that
is shaped like a paddle. The club
comes from New Ireland, which
is an island in the South Seas.

The Egyptians considered a "wedjat eye" (above) a powerful amulet. It is the symbol of Horus, the god of the rising Sun.

The eye within an eye (left) is a watercolor by Jean-Michel Folon, a present-day Belgian artist who also works for magazines, movies, and advertising.

full of mystery.

Eyes can be mirrors . . .

The picture below was painted by Belgian artist René Magritte in 1935. Its title is "The False Mirror." In the picture, the sky is reflected in the eye that is looking at it, just as if it were being seen in a mirror.

and mirrors . . .

In the eye above, a real mirror pretends to be the **pupil**. Contemporary Italian architect Tomaso Buzzi had this eyecatching artwork built into a stone wall.

can be eyes.

Eyes look at us . . .

This scene of the Visitation was painted in the early sixteenth century by an Italian artist named Pontormo. The Visitation is the name given to the visit that Mary, the mother of Jesus, made to her sister Elizabeth when both women were **pregnant**. Elizabeth's child would later be called Saint John the Baptist.

and at each other.

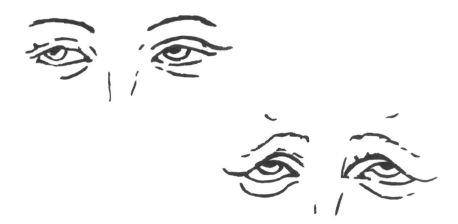

Eyes express . . .

All of these eyes express
different emotions or moods.
They were drawn by French
artist Charles Le Brun, who
lived in the 1600s.

The two Japanese actors in this portrait have extremely expressive eyes. An artist named Sharaku painted the portrait at the end of the eighteenth century.

feelings . . .

and have their own way of speaking.

Casting **telltale** looks at each other, these three cardplayers and the woman serving beverages to them seem to be sending signals with their eyes. The title of this splendid picture is "The Cheat with the Ace of Diamonds." It was painted in the seventeenth century by French artist Georges de La Tour.

GLOSSARY

alabaster
a type of stone used for carving, which is usually white in color and often has bands of other colors running through it

amulet
a charmlike ornament with a figure, symbol, or words on it, which was believed to have magical powers that could protect the wearer from harm, illness, or evils, such as witchcraft

ancient
relating to a period in history from the earliest civilizations until about the time of the Roman Empire

bronze
a hard metal alloy (combination of two or more metals) that is a mixture of mainly copper and tin

cherub
an angel that is often pictured as a chubby and innocent-looking child with wings

contemporary
relating to a person or an event living or happening in current or modern times

depict
to show or describe by means of a picture

divine
heavenly or godlike; belonging to or coming from a god or gods

endowed
given freely as a means of support

figurine
a small, decorative, statuelike figure, usually made of china, pottery, wood, or metal

idol
a figure that symbolizes or represents a god or some other object of worship

Inuit
the Native people, known also as Eskimos, who live in the far northern areas of North America, such as Canada and Alaska, as well as in Greenland and eastern Siberia

ivory
the hard, off-white material that the tusks of elephants and walruses are made of

jade
a hard, green gemstone that is often cut and polished to make figurines

Middle Ages
a period of history in Europe from the end of the Roman Empire to the 1500s

Middle East
a region of the world made up of parts of northeastern Africa, southwestern Asia, and southeastern Europe and which includes countries such as Egypt, Israel, Turkey, Iran, Iraq, and Saudi Arabia

mother-of-pearl
the pearly, rainbowlike lining inside the shells of mollusks such as clams, snails, oysters, and scallops

mythical
based on legends or traditional stories, called myths, rather than on historical facts or events

origins
family beginnings or ancestry

pendant
a type of necklace that is usually a charm or small ornament hanging from a chain

portrait
a picture, photograph, or painting of a person that usually shows just the person's head, neck, and shoulders

pregnant
carrying an unborn child in the womb, which is inside the mother's abdomen

prey
(n) an animal that is hunted and killed by another animal for food

pupil
the dark spot in the iris of a human eye, which opens and closes to control the amount of light entering the eye

stained glass
glass that has been colored by adding various metals and is used to create figures, scenes, and designs for church windows and other decorative objects

statuette
a statue that is usually small enough and lightweight enough to be held in the hands

telltale
giving out information or some kind of recognizable sign

wary
exceptionally watchful and cautious, especially with regard to avoiding danger

watercolor
a painting technique that uses paints or pigments (colorings) that dissolve in water, rather than in oil, often resulting in softer, less defined figures and backgrounds

PICTURE LIST

page 4 – Eye of an animal, from a painted wooden mask. Nootka Indians of Vancouver Island (British Columbia), early 20th century. Seattle, Seattle Art Museum. Drawing by Luigi Ieracitano.

Terra-cotta idol with a head shaped like eyes, from the Eye Temple of Tell Brak (Syria). Sumerian art, 4th millennium B.C. Aleppo, Archaeological Museum. Drawing by Roberto Simoni.

page 5 – Joan Miró (1893-1983): Ciphers and Constellations in Love with a Woman, detail, 1941. Chicago, The Art Institute of Chicago. Museum photo. © Joan Miró by SIAE, 2000.

page 6 – Paul Klee (1879-1940): Senecio, 1922. Basle, Kunsthalle. Photo Scala Archives. © Paul Klee by SIAE, 2000.

page 7 – Wooden ritual mask. Alaska Inuit, late 19th century. Berlin, Ethnographic Museum. Drawing by Luigi Ieracitano.

Jerzy Panek (20th century): Identikit II, woodcut, 1973. Reproduced by courtesy of the publishing house Scheiwiller.

page 8 – Head of a bronze statue of a warrior divinity, from Abini Teti (Sardinia). Nuragic art, 8th century B.C. Drawing Studio Stalio / Alessandro Cantucci.

Painted wooden mask. Art of the Kwele people (Democratic Republic of the Congo). Private property. Drawing by Fiammetta Dogi.

page 9 – Cherub, illumination from an apothropaic scroll. Ethiopian art of the 19th century. London, Sam Fogg Gallery. Drawing by Luigi Ieracitano.

page 10 – "Hei tiki" jade pendant with mother-of-pearl inlays. Maori art, New Zealand, 19th century. Munich, Ethnographic Museum. Drawing by Roberto Simoni.

Alabaster mask in "sultepec" style. Mexican art of the first centuries A.D., from the region of Guerrero. Barcelona, Barbier-Mueller Museum. Drawing by Roberto Simoni.

page 11 – Pablo Picasso (1881-1973): Portrait of woman with striped hat, detail, 1939. Paris, Picasso Museum. Photo RMN. © Pablo Picasso by SIAE, 2000.

page 12 – Dante Gabriel Rossetti (1828-1882): Reverie. Oxford, Ashmolean Museum. Photo Bridgeman / Overseas.

page 13 – Sekine Untei (1804-1877): Head of a tiger. Tokyo, National Museum. Drawing by Luigi Ieracitano.

pages 14-15 – Edvard Munch (1863-1944): The Sun. Oslo, Great Hall of the University. Photo Scala Archives. © Edvard Munch by SIAE, 2000.

page 15 – Stained glass window with face of Christ, from Wissembourg Abbey (Bas-Rhin, France). Alsatian art of the 11th century. Strasbourg, Musée de l'Oeuvre Notre-Dame. Drawing by Luigi Ieracitano.

page 16 – Salvador Dalí (1904-1989): The Eye of Time, 1949. Jeweled watch in blue enamel. Figueres, Fundació Gala-Salvador Dalí. Museum photo. © Salvador Dalí by SIAE, 2000.

page 17 – Detail of a parade helmet, in gold, from Poiana Cotofenesti (Rumania). Thraco-Getic art, 4th century B.C. Bucarest, National Museum. Drawing by Luigi Ieracitano.

Head of a figurine of the goddess Ishtar, in ivory and precious stones. Hellenistic art of Mesopotamia, 4th century B.C. Paris, Louvre. Photo Scala Archives.

page 18 – Jean-Michel Folon (20th century): Somewhere, watercolor, 1975. © Jean-Michel Folon by SIAE, 2000.

Wooden club with two carved eyes. New Ireland (Melanesia, Oceania), early 20th century. Geneva, Barbier-Mueller Museum. Drawing by Fiammetta Dogi.

page 19 – "Wedjat eye," detail of a bracelet in gold, carnelian, and white faience. Egyptian art, early XXII dynasty, 10th century B.C. Cairo, Egyptian Museum. Drawing by Fiammetta Dogi.

page 20 – René Magritte (1898-1967): The False Mirror, 1935. Private property. Photo Photothèque René Magritte – Giraudon / Alinari. © René Magritte by SIAE, 2000.

page 21 – Tomaso Buzzi (1900-1981): Mirror-eye in wall made by Marco Solari. Umbria, Convent of Santa Maria della Scarzuola. Photo Guido Cozzi / Atlantide.

pages 22-23 – Pontormo (1494-1556): Visitation. Carmignano, Church of San Michele. Photo Scala Archives.

page 24 – Charles Le Brun (1619-1690): Expressions of human passions. Drawing by Siriano Nicodemi.

page 25 – Toshusai Sharaku (18th century): Two Actors, colored print. Genoa, Edoardo Chiossone Museum of Oriental Art. Photo Scala Archives.

pages 26-27 – Georges de La Tour (1593-1652): The Cheat with the Ace of Diamonds. Paris, Louvre. Photo Scala Archives.

INDEX

alabaster 10
amulets 10, 19
architects 21
artists 5, 6, 7, 12, 14, 19, 20, 22,
  24, 25, 27

bronze 8
Buzzi, Tomaso 21

carvings 18

Dalí, Salvador 16
de La Tour, Georges 27
drawings 7, 24

emotions (feelings) 24, 25

faces 9, 10, 15, 16
figurines 8
Folon, Jean-Michel 19

gems 16
gods (goddesses) 17, 19

heads 4, 6, 7, 8, 10, 11
helmets 17

idols 4
ivory 17

jade 10

Klee, Paul 6

Le Brun, Charles 24

Magritte, René 20
masks 4, 7, 8
Miró, Joan 5
mirrors 20, 21
mother-of-pearl 10
Munch, Edvard 14

paintings 5, 6, 9, 11, 12, 13, 14,
  20, 22, 25, 27
Panek, Jerzy 7
pendants 10
Picasso 11
Pontormo 22
portraits 12, 25

Rossetti, Dante Gabriel 12
rubies 17

Sharaku 25
stained glass 15
statuettes 17

tigers 13

watercolors 18, 19
wedjat eye 19
women 11, 12, 22, 27